HISTORY'S BIGGEST SHOW-OFFS

The BOLDEST, BRAVEST, & BRAINIEST *people of all time*

By Andy Seed
Illustrated by Sam Caldwell

happy yak

For Proctor—A.S.

For Isla—S.C.

Brimming with creative inspiration, how-to projects, and useful information to enrich your everyday life, quarto.com is a favorite destination for those pursuing their interests and passions.

First Published in 2022 by Happy Yak, an imprint of The Quarto Group.
100 Cummings Center, Suite 265D Beverly, MA 01915, USA.
T (978) 282-9590 F (978) 283-2742
www.quarto.com

Andy Seed has asserted his right to be identified as the author of this work.
Sam Caldwell has asserted his right to be identified as the illustrator of this work.

A CIP record for this book is available from the Library of Congress.

ISBN 978-0-7112-7509-6
eISBN 978-0-7112-7508-9

Designer: Sarah Chapman-Suire
Commissioning Editor: Emily Pither
Editor: Alice Harman
Creative Director: Malena Stojić
Associate Publisher: Rhiannon Findlay
Consultants: Kimberlee Walker and Hester Barron

Manufactured in Singapore COS 072022

9 8 7 6 5 4 3 2 1

Have you seen how much GOLD I have?

Meh, who cares about gold? I'm all about MATH!

The **BOLDEST, BRAVEST, & BRAINIEST** *people of all time*

By Andy Seed

Illustrated by
Sam Caldwell

CONTENTS

PEOPLE IN CHARGE

PEOPLE WHO THINK UP STUFF

PEOPLE WHO CREATE THINGS

Look up the tricky words in the glossary at the back of the book.

Whoa! Look at all those amazing people...

Who shall we read about first?!

MEET THE SHOW-OFFS

To be
or not to be...
A SHOW-OFF!

SHOWING OFF. We've all done it.

Maybe trying to impress our friends, or proving to Granny how fast we can skate (before falling over).

But who are the BIGGEST show-offs of all time?

Who are history's FLASHIEST, LOUDEST, and MOST OUTRAGEOUSLY IMPRESSIVE stars?

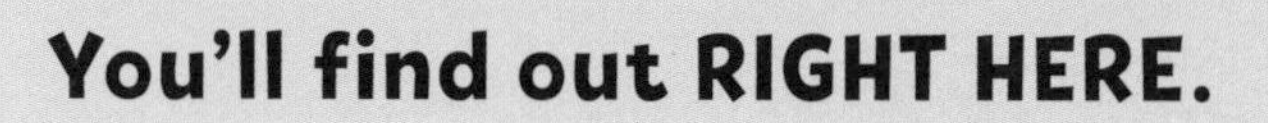

You'll find out RIGHT HERE.

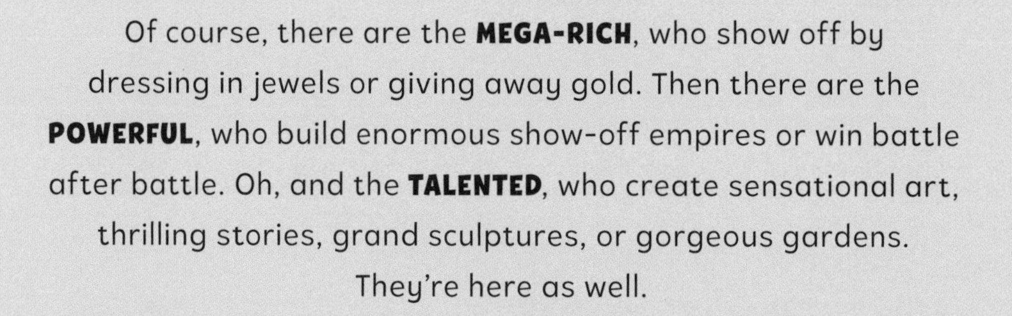

Of course, there are the **MEGA-RICH**, who show off by dressing in jewels or giving away gold. Then there are the **POWERFUL**, who build enormous show-off empires or win battle after battle. Oh, and the **TALENTED**, who create sensational art, thrilling stories, grand sculptures, or gorgeous gardens. They're here as well.

But you can show off by being **EXTRA CLEVER**, too. Like the people in history who built massive structures, dreamed up genius inventions, or solved really hard problems. You can also show off your **INCREDIBLE IMAGINATION**. Like the rebels of the past, who saw the world differently and did things before anyone else. You can read about them here too!

What kind of SHOW-OFF will you be inspired to be?!

CHOOSE YOUR SHOW-OFF JOURNEY!

When you explore this book, you can go on different journeys! If you like, you can simply start the book at the beginning. Or you can jump to the section full of the people you find most interesting—rulers, scientists, or arty types. Or you can look out for the colored tabs at the top of the pages, and check out what show-offs from each period in history got up to:

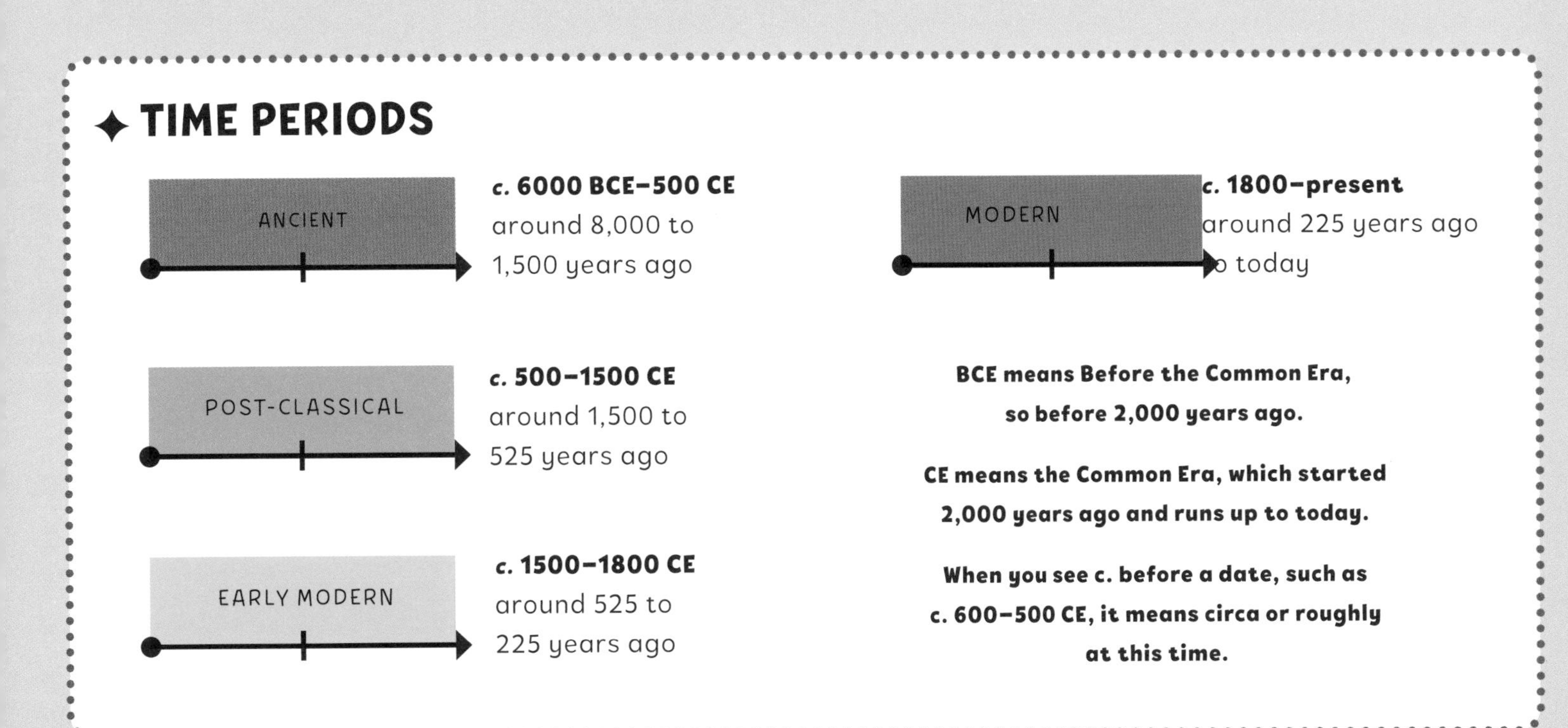

✦ TIME PERIODS

ANCIENT

***c.* 6000 BCE–500 CE**
around 8,000 to 1,500 years ago

POST-CLASSICAL

***c.* 500–1500 CE**
around 1,500 to 525 years ago

EARLY MODERN

***c.* 1500–1800 CE**
around 525 to 225 years ago

MODERN

***c.* 1800–present**
around 225 years ago to today

BCE means Before the Common Era, so before 2,000 years ago.

CE means the Common Era, which started 2,000 years ago and runs up to today.

When you see c. before a date, such as c. 600–500 CE, it means circa or roughly at this time.

✦ ABOUT THE AUTHOR

Andy Seed is not at all a show-off. Well, all right, just a little bit. When not writing books he likes to show off how bad he is at table tennis, how tall he is, and how much he loves cheese, being outdoors, and soccer.

1

PEOPLE IN CHARGE

Imagine being IN CHARGE...
What kind of a ruler would you be?

Some rulers just can't help going **BIG**. *They build* **MASSIVE PALACES** *and put up* **GIANT STATUES** *of themselves. They dress in* **SPARKLY OUTFITS** *and wear enough* **SHINY JEWELS** *to sink a ship! Or they show off their big* **BRAINS**, *and their* **BRAVERY** *in battle.*

➵ Try matching each picture opposite with a name below. Too tricky? Then read about each person in the following pages and come back to show off your matching skills!

1 - *Mansa Musa:* mega-rich ruler who gave away gold

2 - *Mongkut:* busy king and stargazer with a big family

3 - *Tarabai:* brave warrior queen

4 - *Zog:* luxury-loving king who really liked cake

5 - *Hatshepsut:* female ruler of ancient Egypt

6 - *Christina:* brainy, book-loving queen

7 - *Alexander the Great:* leader who took over a huge chunk of the world

8 - *Elizabeth I:* strong and fashionable queen

9 - *Commodus:* nasty Roman emperor who loved to win

10 - *Wu:* empress who wanted power—and got it

11 - *Henry VIII:* king who loved flashy jewelry

Answers on page 62

Female pharaohs
RULE TOO
I love GOLD...
and CAKE
I'm the KING
of BLING
I'm a
FASHION ICON
BRAINS are
BEST!
Want some GOLD?
Ask me!
I'm a BIG
FAMILY man
I'm a
BRAVE BOSS
Riches? Meh.
Power? YEAH!
The world is MINE.
ALL MINE!
I WIN,
you LOSE!
Read on to
find out if you
guessed right
and to really ge
to know these

HATSHEPSUT

In ancient Egypt, it was hard being a female pharaoh. For thousands of years, nearly all the other rulers were men. So when Hatshepsut had her chance to rule, in about 1478 BCE, she WENT FOR IT!

Don't mess with me

Hatshepsut is shown with big, strong shoulders. This is a sign of her power and strength.

Bearded lady?

Male pharaohs were traditionally shown with a BEARD. Hatshepsut wanted to show that she was just as important as them!

Built to last

This carving is about 3,500 years old—pharaohs knew how to show off LONG TERM!

Check out my temple—and my statue! Nice, huh?

Terrific temple

Hatshepsut had an ENORMOUS temple built for the worship of...well, herself! She wanted people to remember her LONG after her death. The temple is decorated with carvings showing Hatshepsut's many achievements. These include opening up trade with the mysterious Land of Punt, where the Egyptians bought everything from gold to baboons!

Going BIG

Hatshepsut had lots of HUGE statues of herself placed around her temple. This one shows her as a magical, lionlike sphinx. Purrrfect show-off style!

TARABAI

In India, in the year 1700, two great kingdoms battled for control of the land. The Mughals had a powerful emperor but the Marathas had a queen with big plans. They both had large armies, forts, and weapons. WHO WOULD WIN?

Who was Tarabai?

Queen Tarabai became leader of the Marathas when her husband died. She was smart, brave, and strong. One writer of the time said she had 'great powers of command'—in other words, she was THE BOSS.

Yeah! Let's show everyone how it's done!

Show us your skills!

Tarabai led the Maratha armies into battle at the age of 25. How did she do it? By showing off her military skills:

- sword fighting
- horse-riding
- archery (bow and arrow)
- clever planning

Going REALLY BIG

Tarabai fought hard for her people and WON! The Marathas beat the Mughals and took over a huge amount of land. Other Maratha rulers added to this, and eventually the Marathas ruled over a MASSIVE area about five times the size of France!

HENRY VIII

King Henry VIII, who ruled England in the 1500s, is probably most famous for his six wives—and the very NASTY way he treated them*. But did you know that he was also a massive SHOW-OFF? He had 55 palaces, held ENORMOUSLY expensive parties, and had LOTS of portraits painted of himself.

What a poser

In 1536, famous artist Hans Holbein painted Henry looking especially proud, tall, and totally royal.

Funnily enough, Henry loved the painting! So much so that he had it copied and sent around Europe, so everyone could see how epic he (thought he) was.

1 Huge Henry

Henry wore shoulder pads to make him look mega-strong and "manly." He also usually appeared in portraits standing with his legs wide apart, probably to make him look tough and powerful. But it might have also helped him not to fall over while wearing all his heavy jewels!

2 Cracking curtains

Even the king's CURTAINS were part of his show-off act! Oh, and carpets—he owned more than 800 of them! His palaces were decorated in the very SWANKIEST styles, to show everyone how royally rich he was.

3 King of bling

Henry LOVED to show off with jewelry, including crowns and heavy chains. Gold and rubies were thought to be his faves.

4 Unusual undies

Believe it or not, underwear as we know it wasn't invented until after Tudor times...so instead of undies, Henry wore a special item called a codpiece.

*** He had two of them killed, and ditched two more (lucky escape for them!)**

2
3
4
1

ELIZABETH I

Queen Elizabeth I of England is one of the most famous and powerful queens of all time. She had many portraits painted of her, and nearly all of them are SHOW-OFF CLASSICS. This one, painted in 1592, is called The Ditchley Portrait.

I wish they'd invent the camera!

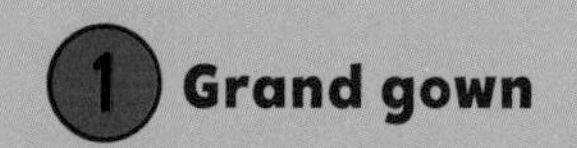

1 Grand gown

The queen's satin and silk dress is simply SPECTACULAR. She is saying LOOK AT ME!

2 Blingtastic

Elizabeth is covered in jewels! Rubies with gold and MONSTER pearls. She's showing off her wealth in style.

3 Storming off

Dark clouds coming? NO WAY! The artist is showing us how this lady can blot out gloom and make the SUN SHINE.

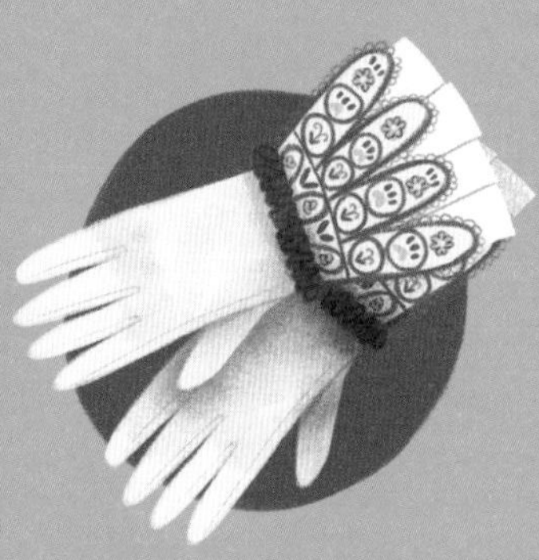

4 Plenty of accessories

Elizabeth liked fancy gloves. In fact, she owned over 2,000 of them. Imagine trying to find a pair to MATCH!

5 The world at her feet

The queen is standing on a globe, with England and Wales at her feet. This is a **symbol** of her great power.

The big picture

The painting is HUGE, much taller than an average adult, making the queen look LARGER than LIFE.

CHRISTINA OF SWEDEN

Some rulers are tough, some are glamorous, and some are DEAD BRAINY. In the 17th century, Queen Christina of Sweden was top of the SMART CHARTS. At the time, women didn't have many opportunities. But, as a queen, Christina had the chance to do a LOT more of what she wanted.

Show-off start

When Christina was crowned queen, she was welcomed with a noisy 1,800 gun salute.

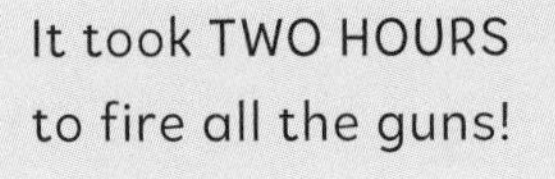

It took TWO HOURS to fire all the guns!

Ready, steady, PAINT

The queen liked to have plenty of new pictures (not of herself!) on display in her royal palace. In the year 1649 alone, she ordered 760 new paintings. You'd need a BIG WALL for all those!

I love learning!

Most girls at the time weren't allowed to go to school. But the queen was educated like a prince, with top-class tutors, and she was VERY enthusiastic about learning:

- she studied for 10 hours a day
- she spoke eight languages
- she was WELL INTO learning Ancient Greek and Latin

When she was older, Christina impressed people with her HUMONGOUS collection of books and science equipment.

TOP TEN!

Gifts given to Queen Elizabeth II

Leaders and rulers often receive fantastic SHOW-OFF gifts. Presents are a great way for other rulers, and sometimes the leader's own people, to SHOW their friendliness and generosity.

Elizabeth II has been Queen of England for over 70 years. In that time, she's been given some VERY INTERESTING things...

1 A CHOCOLATE MODEL OF WINDSOR CASTLE

(UK, 2013)

Luckily, Her Majesty is apparently a big chocolate fan!

2 AN ELEPHANT

(Cameroon, 1972)

The elephant was named Jumbo, and he went to live at London Zoo.

3 500 CANS OF PINEAPPLE

(Australia, 1947)

The cans were given to hungry families in London, where there were food shortages after World War II.

4

A PAINTING OF A SWIMMING PIG

(Bahamas, 2019)

5

A PAIR OF COWBOY BOOTS

(USA, 1991)

6

A POUND OF SALT

(British Virgin Islands, 2015)

It was collected from seaside rock pools on Salt Island.

8

A SLOTH AND TWO JAGUARS

(Brazil, 1968)

10

A MODEL OF PRINCE CHARLES WITH POSTMAN PAT

(Jordan, 2016)

The Postman Pat cartoon has been very popular in Jordan for decades.

7

A BAR OF DOG SOAP

(Australia, 2000)

The Queen is a famous animal lover, and has lots of dogs.

9

A GOLD HORSE COMB

(Slovenia, 2019)

Her Majesty adores horses and has ridden all her life.

KING MONGKUT OF SIAM

The country that we call Thailand was once called Siam. In the 19th century, Siam had a king named Mongkut who was REMARKABLE for many reasons.

Who turned out the lights?

Mongkut studied astronomy, the science of space. In 1868, he had the chance to show off his EPIC SCIENCE SKILLS. He worked out exactly where and when an **eclipse** of the Sun would happen in Siam. And he was RIGHT!

Family fun

At the age of 47, King Mongkut wanted to start a family. Twenty years later, he had 32 WIVES and 82 CHILDREN! That's some family picnic...

Mongkut wanted his huge family to learn English, so he hired a teacher named Anna Leonowens. She wrote a book about her time in Siam, which was later made into a famous musical and film called *The King and I*.

Can't a king get a moment's PEACE?!

KING ZOG OF ALBANIA

Albania's only ever king was named Zog. He started out as a local leader, and eventually became prime minister, then president, and then in the 1920s finally made himself king. There was a LOT of showing off along the way...

Keep the change!

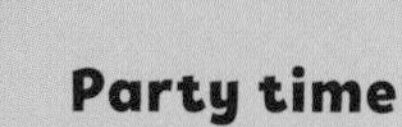

Party time

When Zog finally pushed his way into his new role as king, he threw a HUGE celebration. He declared six days of public holiday, with bonfires and feasts and firing of rockets.

Paying in style

When Italy invaded Albania in 1939, just before World War II, Zog escaped with his large family to Britain. He was helped by Ian Fleming, the famous writer of the James Bond books. Zog stayed at the luxurious Ritz hotel in London, and paid his bill in bars of SOLID GOLD.

What a wedding

In 1938, Zog married Queen Geraldine. Their wedding cake was 10 FEET wide. To take a slice home, you would have needed a VAN!

MANSA MUSA

If anyone can afford to show off, then surely it is THE RICHEST MAN IN HISTORY. He did, and his name was Mansa Musa.

Who WAS he?

Mansa Musa was the ruler of the Kingdom of MALI in Africa in the 1300s. His empire was large and it contained a LOT of gold. It stretched across parts of modern Mali, the country we know today, all the way to the Atlantic Ocean.

The trip of a lifetime

In 1324 Mansa Musa traveled for a YEAR on a very special journey called Hajj...

- As a Muslim, Musa's duty was to visit the holy city of MECCA in Arabia
- He took 60,000 people with him across the Sahara Desert
- His 12,000 servants each carried a LARGE BAG OF GOLD
- Mansa Musa GAVE AWAY the gold as gifts along the way

Was he just generous? Or a show-off?

Mansa Musa wanted people to know that Mali was an important kingdom. He hoped it would bring visitors and trade to his own land. The plan worked!

COMMODUS

Ancient Rome had quite a few emperors who loved showing off, but one of them was a MASTER at it. His name was Commodus and he ruled from 180-192.

Cheat!

Commodus loved sports but he also loved cheating. He always won chariot races because no one was allowed to beat him. He also showed off by pretending to be a gladiator—but all his opponents were ordered to lose...BOO!

Make me a god

The emperor had many large statues of himself put up. But they were NOT realistic—some of the statues showed Commodus as the beefy half-god Hercules. EPIC showing off!

Mr. NOT nice guy

Commodus also loved showing off by "performing" in front of huge crowds. What did he do? He was VERY MEAN and NASTY to lots of animals and people. Boo!

ALEXANDER THE GREAT

Who was the greatest military leader of ALL TIME? Well, this guy never lost a single battle—even against HUGE armies! He was a bit of a STAR when it came to war (and showing off).

✦ YOUNG ✦

In 336 BCE he became KING of Macedonia, in Greece, at the age of 20.

Everyone says I'm "Great"—and I agree!

✦ SUCCESSFUL ✦

He built an army and beat the HUGE Persian Empire, when he was only 25.

✦ BRAVE ✦

He led his troops INTO BATTLE, rather than giving orders from a safe distance.

✦ AMBITIOUS ✦

He wanted to create the BIGGEST EMPIRE IN THE WORLD, and he did!

✦ UNSTOPPABLE ✦

He conquered so many countries that his empire stretched from Greece, throughout the Middle East, into India.

My city, my name!

Alexander didn't just BASH THINGS. He built 70 CITIES all over his empire. Just to show off even more, some were named after him—like Alexandria in Egypt.

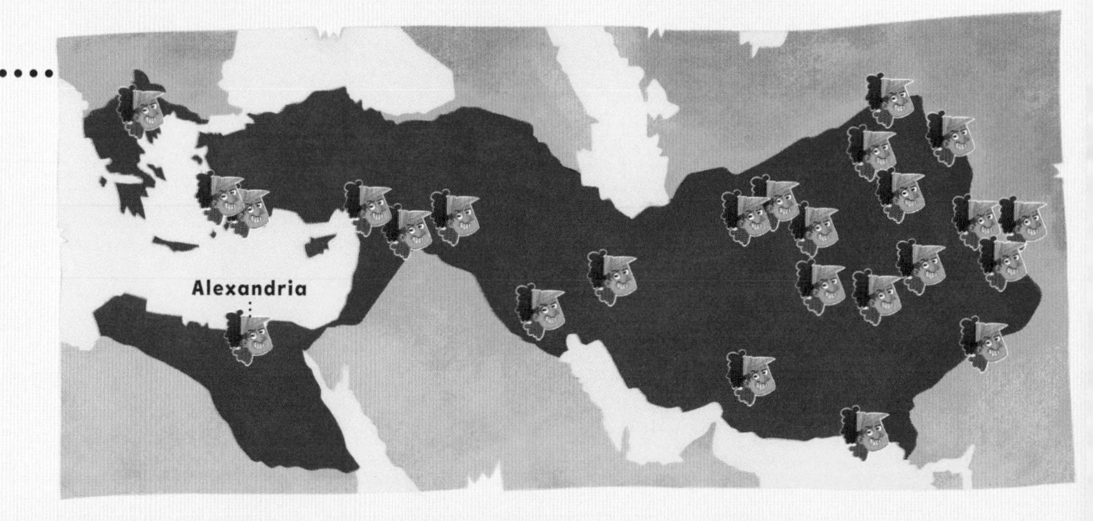

: city named after Alexander the Great

EMPRESS WU

China is a VERY old country and in 3,000 years of history, it has only ever had ONE official female ruler—the remarkable EMPRESS WU.

Who was Wu?

Here are a few essential Empress Wu facts:

- She was born in 624
- She is sometimes known as WU HOU or WU ZETIAN
- She was a ruler in the TANG Dynasty
- She held power for OVER 50 YEARS!

What did she do as ruler?

LOTS! First of all, she ruled a country of 50 million people for decades. She showed off her great POWER by expanding her empire and helping China to become VERY RICH. She also built temples, wrote poetry, and supposedly caused her enemies to MYSTERIOUSLY DIE...

Have you ever tried running an enormous country? I deserve to show off a bit!

China

Great names

Wu was awarded many fabulous SHOW-OFF TITLES, including:

- TALENTED LADY
- HEAVENLY EMPRESS
- HOLY GOLDEN GODDESS EMPEROR

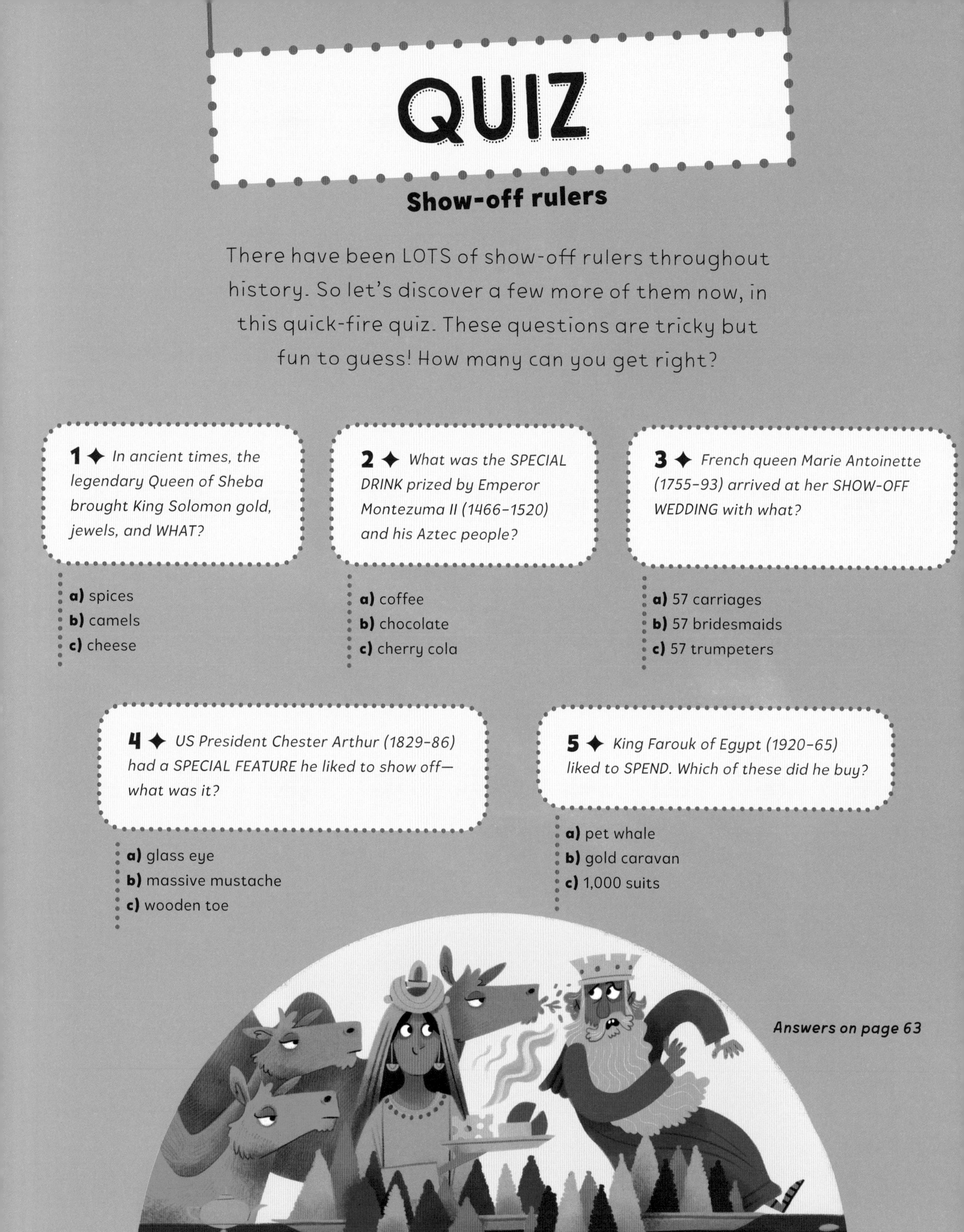

QUIZ

Show-off rulers

There have been LOTS of show-off rulers throughout history. So let's discover a few more of them now, in this quick-fire quiz. These questions are tricky but fun to guess! How many can you get right?

1 ✦ *In ancient times, the legendary Queen of Sheba brought King Solomon gold, jewels, and WHAT?*

- **a)** spices
- **b)** camels
- **c)** cheese

2 ✦ *What was the SPECIAL DRINK prized by Emperor Montezuma II (1466–1520) and his Aztec people?*

- **a)** coffee
- **b)** chocolate
- **c)** cherry cola

3 ✦ *French queen Marie Antoinette (1755–93) arrived at her SHOW-OFF WEDDING with what?*

- **a)** 57 carriages
- **b)** 57 bridesmaids
- **c)** 57 trumpeters

4 ✦ *US President Chester Arthur (1829–86) had a SPECIAL FEATURE he liked to show off—what was it?*

- **a)** glass eye
- **b)** massive mustache
- **c)** wooden toe

5 ✦ *King Farouk of Egypt (1920–65) liked to SPEND. Which of these did he buy?*

- **a)** pet whale
- **b)** gold caravan
- **c)** 1,000 suits

Answers on page 63

✦ WHAT ABOUT YOU? ✦

If you were ruler for a day,
what would you choose?

Palace OR castle?

Huge yacht OR private jet?

Lavish party OR tour of your tropical island?

Gold shoes OR diamond sunglasses?

Your own horse to ride OR hundreds of pets?

Be NICE!

If you were king or queen, what would you do for ORDINARY PEOPLE?

Vote for me!

How would you convince people to vote you into power? Try making up a short speech about the world-changing things you'd do as a ruler.

2 PEOPLE WHO THINK UP STUFF

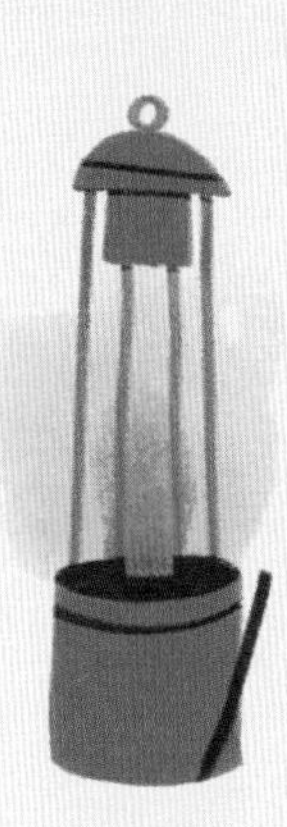

Imagine being an INVENTOR or a SCIENTIST. What would you make or discover?

*Some people are **SO SMART** that they can't help showing off their ideas. They invent **MEGA MACHINES** and exciting **NEW TECH**. Or they do **DARING EXPERIMENTS** and discover new substances or ways to **MAKE LIFE BETTER** for people.*

➾ Try matching each picture opposite with a name below. Too tricky? Then read about each person in the following pages and come back to show off your matching skills!

1 - ***Ada Lovelace:*** first ever computer programmer

2 - ***Antoine Lavoisier:*** scientist who discovered the gases oxygen and hydrogen

3 - ***Montgolfier Brothers:*** built the first flying machine

4 - ***Humphry Davy:*** gave fiery science talks

5 - ***Marie Curie:*** prize-winning, life-saving super-scientist

6 - ***Hedy Lamarr:*** film star and ace tech inventor

7 - ***Ynes Mexia:*** plant collector and epic traveler

8 - ***Thomas Edison:*** inventor and businessman with lots of ideas

9 - ***Nikola Tesla:*** master of electrical inventions

10- ***Isambard Kingdom Brunel:*** bold engineer who liked to build big things

Answers on page 62

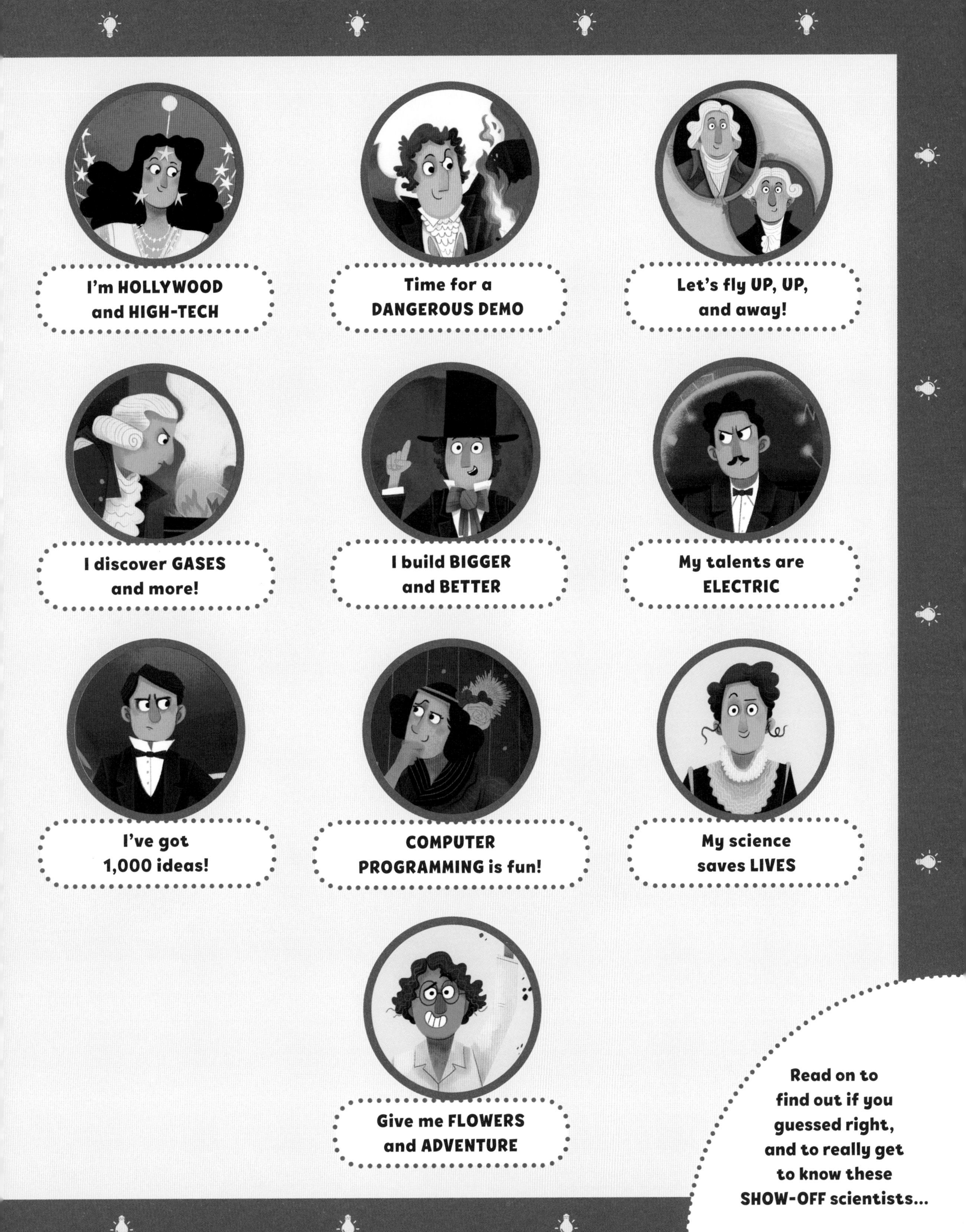
I'm HOLLYWOOD and HIGH-TECH
Time for a DANGEROUS DEMO
Let's fly UP, UP, and away!
I discover GASES and more!
I build BIGGER and BETTER
My talents are ELECTRIC
I've got 1,000 ideas!
COMPUTER PROGRAMMING is fun!
My science saves LIVES
Give me FLOWERS and ADVENTURE
Read on to find out if you guessed right, and to really get to know these SHOW-OFF scientists...

ADA LOVELACE

In the 1840s, there was no such device as a computer. Scientists were inventing machines to do calculations, but it took a GENIUS young English woman to fully understand what else they could do.

Fancy family

Ada was VERY FANCY. She was the daughter of zany poet Lord Byron, a huge celeb in the early 19th century. In 1835 she married a rich earl and became a countess, but Ada was more interested in MATH than money!

I'd rather PROGRAM than party!

How did she show off?

At the time, women were not taken seriously in science and math, but Ada had just as much understanding and imagination as the clever men of her day. It was DARING for her to share her ideas and show off her EPIC BRAIN POWER!

Babbling with Babbage

Ada met a brainy inventor named Charles Babbage who had made plans for a big CALCULATING MACHINE to crunch numbers. But Ada saw that the machine could be instructed to do all kinds of things. She wrote down her ideas, and in her notes was the world's first ever COMPUTER PROGRAM. Wow!

ANTOINE LAVOISIER

Oxygen is a REALLY handy gas. For a start, we need it to breathe! But for hundreds of years, no one knew that it was part of air. Then, in the 18th century, a very clever French scientist worked it all out. What a BREATHtaking discovery!

Show-off science

Lavoisier came from a wealthy family and could afford to do pretty much anything he liked, so he built his own lab to do experiments. He worked with gunpowder and caused a LOT of explosions.

Hey, I've invented chemistry...

As well as naming oxygen and hydrogen (another handy, invisible gas), Antoine identified another 53 chemical elements. That's almost half of the 118 elements that we know about today!

Getting the chop

Lavoisier was also a tax collector, which made him even richer. But then came the French Revolution, a time of great change. The king was removed, and the new leaders didn't like rich, flashy tax collectors AT ALL. In 1794, they chopped off Lavoisier's head. It's hard to do experiments without one...

THE MONTGOLFIER BROTHERS

If you want to show off your flashy new invention, then why not do it in front of the KING and QUEEN? Especially if you've invented something as impressive as a FLYING MACHINE!

Bonjour!

Je suis Jacques!

Ballooning bros

- Joseph and Jacques Montgolfier were brothers, born in France.
- There were 16 kids in their family!
- The brothers were ace INVENTORS, and made the first successful hot-air balloon in 1783.

The Montgolfier brothers' invention was the HOT-AIR BALLOON.At the magnificent Palace of Versailles near Paris they showed off how it worked in front of the King of France, Louis XVI (the 16th), and his wife, Marie Antoinette.

A quacking idea

The brothers were not sure if it was safe for humans to fly—no one had ever done it before! So they sent three animals into the air first: a duck, a sheep, and a rooster.

Happy heroes

The farmyard trio rose 2,000 feet upward in a basket tied beneath the balloon. They drifted above the city for over 2 miles before landing in a wood. All three animals were celebrated as heroes, later becoming part of the king's private zoo!

Duck! There's a fire over our heads!

Cock-a-doodle don't!

This is baaaad!

Going up in the world

Joseph's and Jacques's next balloon carried two people over Paris for 25 minutes. It was the first ever human flight and they REALLY went for a show-off look! The new balloon was bright blue with gold suns, eagles, and all kinds of FANCY BITS. It even had the King's face on it!

HOW DID IT WORK?

1. A fire was lit under the balloon.
2. This made lots of hot air, which is lighter than cold air, so it rises.
3. The hot air filled the balloon, making it rise.
4. When the air cooled, the balloon slowly descended.

MARIE CURIE

In late 19th-century Europe, scientists were pretty much all men. Until Marie Curie SWOOPED in and proved to the world just how impressively smart she was, winning her well-earned place in science history.

I'm full of scientific CURIE-osity. Ha. Ha. Ha.

This is NEW!

Marie worked EXTREMELY hard and discovered two chemical elements never seen before. She called them polonium and radium. People were amazed by her work and she was given COOL MEDALS.

Doubly brilliant

In the early 20th century, Marie Curie became the first woman ever to win a NOBEL PRIZE, the top award in science. In fact, she won TWO! This SPECTACULAR show-off proved that women can be SUPER scientists.

Glow in the dark

Curie found out that radium gives off rays of heat and light. It even glows in the dark! She called this "radioactivity." Her discoveries led to the use of X-rays by doctors, and a way to fight cancer. Her work still helps to SAVE LIVES today!

HUMPHRY DAVY

Davy was a gifted inventor who enjoyed showing off science to ordinary people. In 1801 in London, he gave his first big talk to the public, showing off some of his dramatic experiments with chemicals. They LOVED it!

Dangerous Davy

Humphry was a real showman and he loved blowing things up. He even set DIAMONDS alight! It was NOT safe to be near him, and in 1812 he lost his sight for a few weeks after a chemical blast.

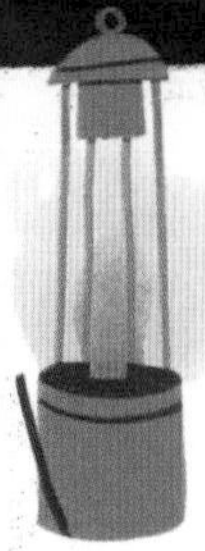

Light work

Davy invented a special lamp for miners to use while working underground. It had a metal mesh screen around the flame inside. It was safer than candles, whose flames could light the gases underground and cause explosions.

Paid to show off

Humphry was paid to give public lectures about science. Big crowds turned up and he wowed them with loud bangs, colorful clouds of gases and LOTS of setting fire to things.

TOP FIVE!

Inventions that wowed the world

Many inventors LOVE showing off their new inventions, and we like to think that most ideas come from one VERY SMART person working alone in a SHED. But that almost NEVER happens. Mostly, over time, lots of people IMPROVE an invention until it works really well. Here are five of the most useful inventions ever.

Bet I can fly this to the top of a pyramid!

1 POTTERY

(about 20,000 years ago)

How did you carry water before containers were invented? It was VERY HARD. Then someone discovered that if you put a clay jar in a VERY HOT fire, it becomes hard and strong. You have a pot!

2 PAPER

(about 4,500 years ago)

Paper is SO useful. I mean, how did people live without it? No paper = NO BOOKS, arrghh! But then the brainy ancient Egyptians learned how to make papyrus from plant stems, and paper was born!

The Chinese improved paper a lot, too, by smushing up RAGS together with plant materials.

So THAT's where I am!

Oops, wrong number!

3 ✦ THE COMPASS

(about 2,200 years ago)

In times of OLD, sailors were always getting lost at sea. Then someone in China found a MAGNETIC ROCK (lodestone) that points north to south when dangled from a string.

Middle Eastern and European inventors made it work even better, using a magnetic needle in a bowl of water. Handy!

4 ✦ THE PRINTING PRESS

(about 600 years ago)

Making books was RIDICULOUSLY SLOW before 1440. Copies had to be made by hand and it took AGES.

Then a German dude named Gutenberg built a wooden printing machine, using ideas from China and Korea. It was WAY, WAY faster. Today, printers are EVERYWHERE.

5 ✦ THE TELEPHONE

(about 150 years ago)

For most of history, the idea that you could TALK to someone far away was considered HILARIOUS.

But by the 19th century, discoveries and inventions using electricity, wires, magnets, and more helped inventors to make REALLY exciting things happen. In 1876, a guy gave someone a ring for the first time. His name was BELL!

YNES MEXIA

In 1925, a woman decided to start collecting and studying as many different plants as she could from wild places in North and South America. Her name was Ynes Mexia, she was 56 years old, and she was AMAZING.

I'm glad plant collecting is such a safe job.

Going it alone

Ynes traveled thousands of miles alone, looking for rare plants on mountains, in deserts, and in freezing valleys. She explored places including Alaska, Brazil, Peru, Chile, and Mexico (where her family came from). She even spent over TWO YEARS sailing and canoeing up 3,100 miles of the Amazon River!

Watch out!

There were lots of dangers in the wild places that Ynes visited. She once fell off a cliff reaching for a plant, and broke several bones. Another time she was trapped on a dog sled in a snowstorm.

Big SHOW-OFF numbers

Ynes became a world expert on plants. In just 13 years, she...

- collected 145,000 plants to study
- discovered 500 NEW SPECIES
- had 50 plants named after her!

HEDY LAMARR

When you hear the word "inventor," do you imagine a quiet person working alone in a lab? Well, SURPRISE! All kinds of people are inventors—even HOLLYWOOD FILM STARS! Like Hedy Lamarr...

A star is born

Lamarr was born in Austria and wanted to be an actor. She starred in her first film when she was still a teenager. She moved to Paris, then London, then Hollywood. She was a talented actor and appeared in lots of American films. By the 1940s she had become a glamorous, world-famous movie star!

I'm BORED

Hedy had a BRILLIANT BRAIN and she got a bit bored being famous, although she loved showing off her acting skills. So she started inventing things—and she was AWESOME at that, too!

Who said you had to choose between science and GLAMOR?

Ahead of her time

Working with a friend, Hedy invented a way for ships to guide weapons using radio, to help win World War II. Her high-tech ideas were later used in making Wi-Fi and Sat Nav technology, which we use today!

In the 1890s in the USA, buildings were lit by candles or gas lamps. The light bulb had been invented, but who would figure out how to get ELECTRICITY into homes and offices? The race was on, and two top SHOW-OFF INVENTORS battled it out.

THE BATTLE OF

In the left corner: THOMAS EDISON!

Ingenious inventor!

Smart businessman!

NO ONE out-invents ME

Why was Edison FAMOUS?

- He made an electric light bulb (that actually worked well!)
- He invented the record player
- He invented the movie camera
- He held the world record for most inventions (over 1,000!)

Science that sells

Edison was a famous American inventor. Not all of his inventions were good (he made concrete furniture!) but he came up with a HUGE number of them. He was also a WHIZ when it came to selling his ideas.

He was very good at showing off how his new devices worked, and the newspapers LOVED him because he was always coming up with something new and clever.

THE SHOW-OFFS

My inventions are SHOCKINGLY good

In the right corner:
NIKOLA TESLA!
Engineer!
Inspirational inventor!

Why was Tesla FAMOUS?

- He made a power supply system that carried ELECTRICITY over long distances. It was much better than Edison's system—and it's still used today
- He built a generator that was powered by NIAGARA FALLS: clean, green energy!
- He invented lots of other electrical devices, such as RADIO

All about the science

Serbian-American inventor Tesla's electrical innovations were totally GENIUS and way ahead of their time. He AMAZED audiences by making flashes of electricity that looked like LIGHTNING! Unlike Edison, he wasn't really interested in fame and fortune, and he ended up losing most of his money. Many inventors today are INSPIRED by him, though—there is even a famous make of ELECTRIC CAR called the Tesla!

SHOW-OFF RATING

- **INVENTING skills** 10
- **Getting RICH** 5
- **Fabulously FAMOUS** 7

ISAMBARD KINGDOM BRUNEL

In Britain in the 1800s, the aim was to BUILD BUILD BUILD! People wanted the newly invented railways, as well as huge bridges, tunnels, and steam ships. Who could SHOW OFF their talent making all of those? The greatest ENGINEER of his day, that's who!

Crossing the gorge

In the city of Bristol in England, the River Avon cuts a deep gorge between high cliffs. To get people across the river, Bristol needed a bridge. A young man named Isambard came up with an impressive SHOW-OFF design for a suspension bridge, where the road hangs from cables fixed to towers.

That's GORGE-ous!

Clifton classic

Brunel's Clifton Suspension Bridge took 33 years to finish building, with LONG pauses when the project ran out of money. Brunel actually died before it was completed! But the bridge is still standing strong today, and more than 4 MILLION cars and other vehicles use it each year.

Railway fever

In Brunel's time, the usual way to carry people and things was by horse and cart. It was SO SLOW. Then WHIZZY trains came along! Brunel designed the Great Western Railway from London to Cornwall, with HUGE tunnels and bridges. People loved it!

Sea that?

Next, Brunel wanted to show that he could make a giant STEAMSHIP to cross the great ATLANTIC OCEAN to New York. He built THREE, one made of wood and two made of metal. Each one was the biggest ship in the world, meaning he broke his OWN record twice. Now that is showing off!

Walking under the THAMES

Isambard and his father, Marc, built the first ever tunnel under a river. It was designed to help people cross London's wide RIVER THAMES, as tall ships made building bridges tricky. The tunnel took 18 difficult years and lots of clever new TECH to build. When it was finished, tourists LOVED it—there were even underground parties and a FAIRGROUND!

QUIZ

Show-off engineers and inventors

There have been LOTS of genius engineers and inventors throughout history. So let's discover a few more of them now, in this quick-fire quiz. These questions are tricky but fun to guess!

1 ✦ *In 1829, British engineer George Stephenson (1781–1848) built a famous machine called ROCKET. What was it?*

a) rocket
b) car
c) railway locomotive

2 ✦ *The Banu Musa brothers, who lived in Baghdad in the 9th century, were GENIUS engineers! What did they invent?*

a) shape-shifting fountains
b) yogurt maker
c) exploding pants

3 ✦ *Eight hundred years ago, a Muslim engineer named Al-Jazari (1136–1206) wrote a book, full of 50 inventions that showed off his ACE ideas. Can you guess which of these was in the book?*

a) flying car
b) robot band that played music
c) mobile phone

4 ✦ *In 1883, Emily Warren Roebling (1843–1903) helped to build BROOKLYN BRIDGE in New York, the longest suspension bridge in the world. What did she do to celebrate finishing the bridge?*

a) bungee-jumped off it
b) rode across it with a rooster on her knee
c) blew a raspberry at it

5 ✦ *Marie Van Brittan Brown (1922–1999) was a nurse and inventor. What was she the first person to invent, in the 1960s?*

a) electric lawnmower
b) flat-screen TV
c) home security system

Answers on page 62

✦ WHAT ABOUT YOU? ✦

Device dream

If you were a top inventor, what SHOW-OFF MACHINE would you make?

Build bold

If you were a stylish engineer, what shiny new SHOW-OFF TRANSPORT SYSTEM would you design?

✦ INVENTIONS OF THE FUTURE ✦

Which would you choose?

Can you come up with your own futuristic invention?

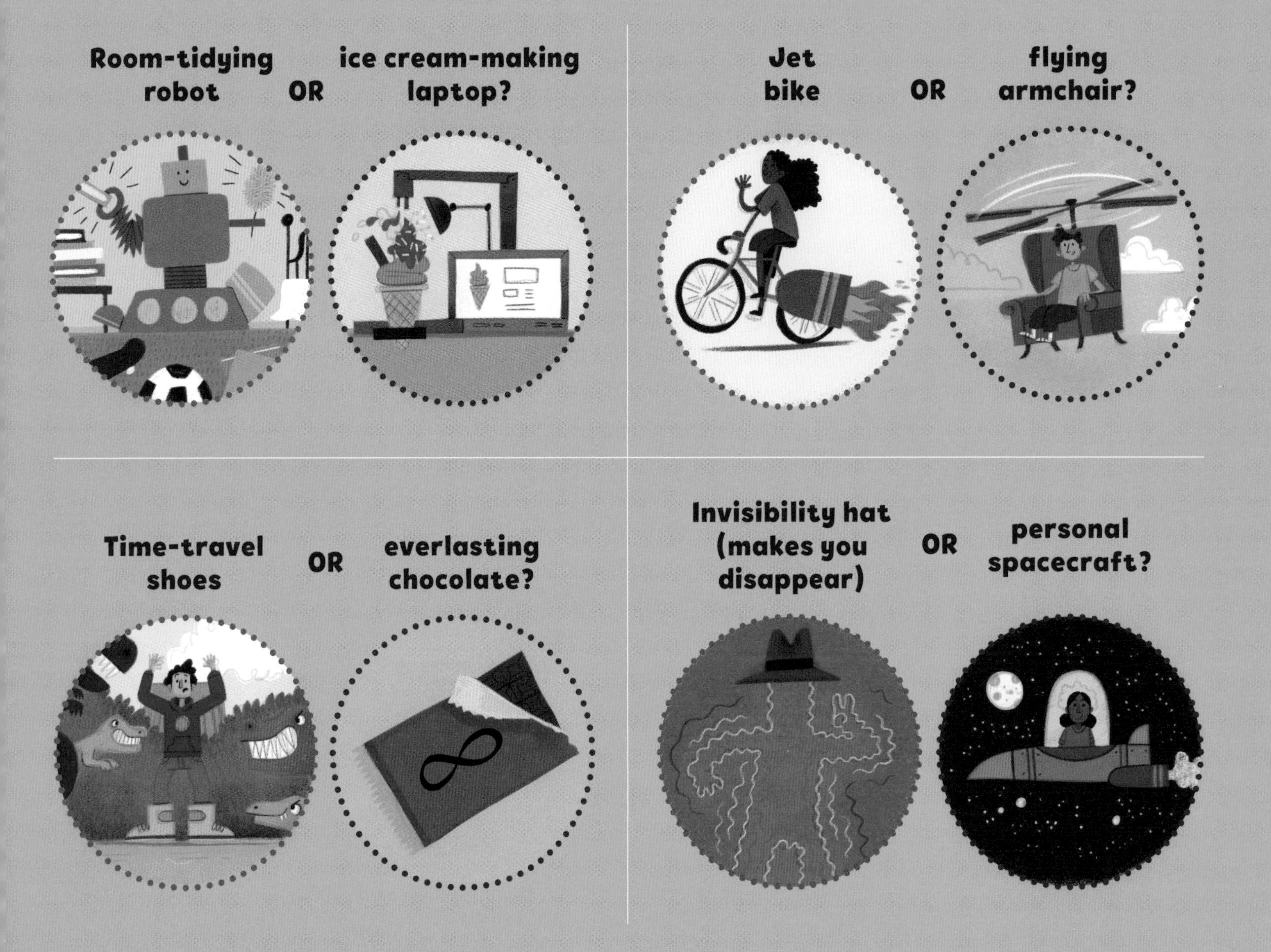

3 PEOPLE WHO CREATE THINGS

Imagine being an ARTISTIC or CREATIVE GENIUS.
What would you do or make?

Some people have so much **SKILL** *and* **TALENT** *that they simply have to show it off! They paint* **STUNNING PICTURES** *or carve* **GRAND STATUES**. *They cook* **DELICIOUS FOOD** *and write* **WONDERFUL BOOKS** *or* **PLAYS**. *Or they create* **BEAUTIFUL BUILDINGS** *and* **GORGEOUS GARDENS**.

QUIZ
WHO'S WHO?

➼ Try matching each picture opposite with a name below. Too tricky? Then read about each person in the following pages and come back to show off your matching skills!

1 - ***Frida Kahlo:*** Mexican artist and fashion sensation

2 - ***Michelangelo:*** amazing painter and sculptor of big, beautiful statues

3 - ***Sophie Taeuber-Arp:*** multi-talented painter, designer, and craftsperson

4 - ***Salvador Dalí:*** made strange, tricky paintings (and sculptures)

5 - ***Jean-Michel Basquiat:*** artist who filled galleries and street walls with art

6 - ***Capability Brown:*** royal gardener and landscape designer

7 - ***Manchu-Han Imperial Feast chefs:*** creators of a giant feast

8 - ***Ustad Ahmad Lahori:*** architect of the Taj Mahal, a beautiful world wonder

9 - ***Antoni Gaudí:*** creator of big, colorful buildings

10 - ***William Shakespeare:*** writer of some of history's most famous plays

11 - ***Oscar Wilde:*** witty, fashionable writer who threw fun parties

Answers on page 62

I paint, craft, build, AND design!

I like to design BIG and COLORFUL buildings

I love plays, O YAY!

My beautiful BUILDING is a world wonder

I paint with the colors of MEXICO

I make GRAND gardens

I like pics with TRICKS!

My WRITING and PARTIES are top-notch

I make art for the STREET and for fancy GALLERIES

My statues are BIG and BEAUTIFUL

All you can eat—AND MORE!

Read on to find out if you guessed right, and to really get to know these SHOW-OFF creatives...

FRIDA KAHLO

Frida Kahlo was a Mexican artist who painted unique pictures in the 1930s, '40s, and, '50s. Her favorite subject? HERSELF! She proudly showed her colorful style and Mexican heritage in her clothes, her hairstyles, and her art, and became a FASHION SENSATION.

Life-changing moments

When Kahlo was just 18, she was on a bus when it crashed. She was seriously injured, and broke her back. After the accident, she was often in SEVERE PAIN for the rest of her life. She walked with a limp, and later in life she used a wheelchair.

Kahlo had to spend a LONG time recovering in bed after the accident, and she got BORED. To pass the time, she took up PAINTING. And she wasn't just good at it—she was AMAZING. There wasn't much to see lying flat in bed, though, so her mom put up a mirror over the bed. Now Frida had a subject for her paintings—her own FACE!

Powerful portraits

Frida often painted herself wearing traditional MEXICAN CLOTHING, and staring straight out at the viewer. Her paintings are also full of ANIMALS, PLANTS, strong EMOTIONS, myths and MAGIC, and strange SYMBOLS—objects that represent her ideas or parts of her life.

Stand-out style

Frida's traditional clothes from North and Central America often included:

- bright blouses
- long colorful skirts
- silky scarves
- huge chunky necklaces
- flowers and ribbons in her hair

Success and SENSATION!

In 1938, Kahlo's paintings went on display in a GALLERY in New York. It was a big success! She sold many pictures, including four to a FILM STAR named Edward G. Robinson! Many fashionable people also noticed the colorful Mexican dress that she wore. They said she was SENSATIONAL and wanted to dress like her.

I want to look like THAT!

After Kahlo died, in 1954, she became a FASHION ICON known around the world. Today, people still love her bold style but it's her astounding ART that she is most remembered for.

MICHELANGELO

Once in a while, a person comes along who is so INCREDIBLY TALENTED that everything they do seems to be showing off. They're so great that it's UNFAIR! The artist, poet, and architect Michelangelo, born in Italy around 550 years ago, was one of these people.

Was it good? Was it big?

Michelangelo's sculpture of David was BREATHTAKING (and still is). The people loved it. It's HUGE—16.5 feet tall, almost three times the size of the average man—and it took Michelangelo three years to carve it out of marble. Oh, and David has NO CLOTHES ON!

He could have at least given me some PANTS.

Going big

The bosses of Florence, an important city in what is now Italy, wanted a statue to show off their POWER and WEALTH. Michelangelo said, "Well, I can make you a GIANT sculpture of King David from the Bible." They replied, "Oooh, yes PLEASE!"

Time to paint the ceiling...

Michelangelo loved to SHOW OFF his incredible painting skills, too. In Rome, church leaders asked him to paint Bible scenes on the ceiling of the 130-foot-long Sistine Chapel. It took four years and is one of the world's GREATEST works of art.

I'm going to need a REALLY long brush.

SOPHIE TAEUBER-ARP

Some people are good at drawing and painting. Some are good at sewing. Others are good at making chairs or writing or dancing or decorating rooms. Could anyone be good at ALL OF THEM?!

Idea explosion!

Taeuber-Arp was always BURSTING WITH IDEAS and the range of her talents was SENSATIONAL. She loved to experiment and try out new ways of making pictures and objects, using all sorts of ARTS and CRAFTS. She wasn't interested in making realistic pictures of things. Instead, she played around with SHAPE and COLOR and PATTERN. Taeuber-Arp's exciting work is now on display around the world.

painting

making costumes

making furniture

making puppets

designing buildings

Who's the Dada?

Sophie, who was from Switzerland, joined other artists in Europe who wanted to do NEW and DIFFERENT things. Together, they created an art movement called DADA. They liked wacky ideas, nonsense, chaos, and fun—all to get people talking and thinking.

THE BATTLE OF

The world of ART is always changing. In the 1920s and 1930s, artists such as Salvador Dalí became famous trying out new, exciting ideas. But by the 1980s, a new generation of bright, young artists—such as Jean-Michel Basquiat—were bringing art from the STREET into fancy galleries.

In the left corner:

SALVADOR DALI!

Imaginative painter!

Quirky style icon!

I make pics with tricks!

Why was Dalí FAMOUS?

- He paintings were like strange dreams, with weird animals and figures
- He had a pointy mustache and dressed in exotic ways
- He loved shocking people—for example, by turning up at events with an anteater!
- He played around with clever visual tricks in his art

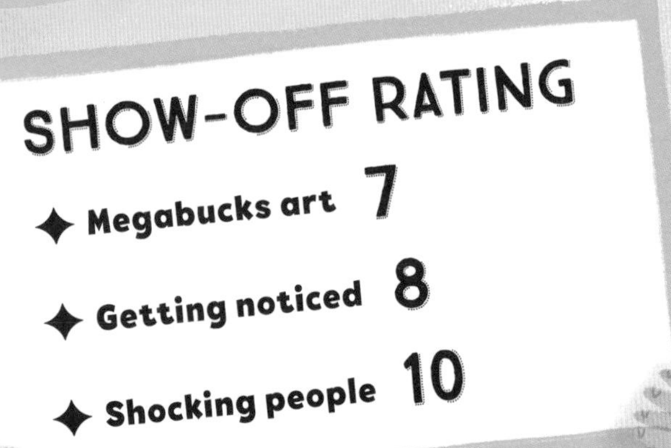

Playful painter

Dalí was a very talented painter from Spain, and his art was far from ordinary. His odd, dreamlike paintings and sculptures featured elephants, eggs, and melting clocks. He also used tricks such as optical illusions, where one thing looks like another.

This style was called Surrealism and it had first become popular in the 1920s. It definitely got people talking! Within a few decades, though, the art world had moved on.

THE SHOW-OFFS

If you want a painting, start saving NOW!

In the right corner: **JEAN-MICHEL BASQUIAT!**

Hugely talented art star!

Young experimental graffiti artist!

Why was Basquiat FAMOUS?

- His art was edgy, different, and exciting, full of new ideas and complex meanings
- As a young Black artist in the USA, he brought a different point of view to a mostly white art world
- He was COOL! He loved fashion and often wore paint-splattered luxury suits with bare feet
- He worked with the Pop Art legend Andy Warhol

Success!

In 1980s New York, art galleries were looking for new talent. Basquiat's pictures were loud, different, full of energy, and sometimes frightening. This style was called Neo-expressionism. He was one of the few Black artists on the new art scene who "broke through" into the big-money art world.

Salvador Dalí's top artworks have sold for over $20,000,000 (twenty million dollars) but Basquiat's have gone for over $100,000,000 (one hundred million dollars)!

SHOW-OFF RATING

- **Megabucks art** 10
- **Getting noticed** 8
- **Shocking people** 7

CAPABILITY BROWN

Brown was an inventive landscape designer in 1750s Britain who made ENORMOUS gardens for lords, dukes, and earls. These gardens looked like beautiful stretches of countryside, and their wealthy owners LOVED them.

We'll just move those hills, pop in a big lake, and build a bridge. Simple!

Brown's big plans

Brown started out as an ordinary gardener, but he was talented and had BIG PLANS. His ideas became so FASHIONABLE that he was made Royal Gardener for King George III at Hampton Court Palace.

BIG jobs

Making huge SHOW-OFF gardens (some as big as 1,000 soccer fields) was not easy!

- some gardens took over 10 years to finish
- Brown made lakes, moved rivers, built bridges, and even created small hills
- there were no diggers or machinery to use
- each project needed hundreds of workers
- workers planted thousands of trees

Call me Lance

Brown's real first name was Lancelot, but he told his rich clients that their estates had CAPABILITY (potential) for improvement. That became his nickname!

THE MANCHU-HAN FEAST

Picture a show-off meal so HUGE that it takes THREE DAYS to eat! Is this REAL? Is this POSSIBLE? The story goes that around 350 years ago, one Chinese emperor held possibly the GREATEST BANQUET IN HISTORY, called the Manchu-Han Imperial Feast.

Meaty menus

Guests supposedly feasted on more than 100 dishes, made by the finest chefs. They included:

- camel's hump
- shark's fin
- bear's paw
- monkey brains
- gorilla lips

A legendary lunch...

The emperor supposedly held the lunch to help bring together rival clans from different parts of his country. If you had an invite, you'd better be HUNGRY!

Hmm, maybe having a snack so close to dinner wasn't such a good idea...

Fabulous feasts

Many restaurants have tried to recreate this legendary feast. In 1977, a TV channel hired 160 CHEFS to make a modern version of the feast, using different ingredients.

TOP FIVE!

You want a groovy way to show off? Then go for MUSIC! Lots of people sing or play instruments but some do it with STYLE, SWAGGER and TOTAL BRILLIANCE. Here are five people from the last 2,000 years whose gigs were spectacular!

Marvelous Musicians

1 MOZART

There is musical greatness, there is musical GENIUS, then there is WOLFGANG AMADEUS MOZART, born in 1756. How good was he? Well, he started learning the keyboard at the age of three. He was a good player by four. By five he was composing his own music! At age six he was giving concerts for ROYALTY. He wrote his first symphony at just eight!

He was a SENSATIONAL piano and violin player. As an adult, he went on to create more than 600 pieces of music.

2 KASSIA

You have to be a REALLY GOOD musician to still be remembered 1,000 YEARS after you die! Kassia lived in the 800s, in what is now called Turkey.

As a woman, she found it hard to get her hymns and songs noticed, but they were SO GOOD that they are still performed today! She was a NUN in charge of a convent, too—not your USUAL SHOW-OFF but she was way ahead of her time!

3 PIXINGUINHA

In 1920s Brazil, Pixinguinha (pronounced Pish-in-GUI-nia) developed a whole NEW STYLE of music. With his band, he made a new version of the music called choro, blending traditional Brazilian songs with American Jazz and music from across the African continent.

People all over the world LOVED it! As well as writing songs, Pixinguinha played the flute, piano, AND saxophone—what a talented show-off!

4 MARIA CALLAS

Who is the greatest female opera singer of all time? Many say it was Maria Callas, a Greek soprano who started performing for audiences at just FIVE years old!

She had a BEAUTIFUL, POWERFUL voice, and became a huge star in the 1950s, traveling the world to perform for thrilled audiences. She was also a very good actor on stage. Altogether, a Callas-ic talent!

5 FATS WALLER

In 1930s USA, the COOLEST music around was JAZZ. One of the best jazz piano players and singers was Fats Waller, a funny and creative man who wrote more than 400 songs. He appeared in a number of HOLLYWOOD MOVIES and also wrote some hit musical shows.

Fats Waller was such an in-demand musician and entertainer that he was once KIDNAPPED by gangsters to play at a birthday party for their boss!

USTAD AHMAD LAHORI

Imagine being asked to create THE MOST BEAUTIFUL BUILDING IN THE WORLD. Well, around 400 years ago, that's just what Ustad Ahmad Lahori was asked to do!

A love story

Shah Jahan was the emperor of the mighty Mughal Empire, which covered most of modern-day India and Pakistan. He loved his wife Mumtaz very much. When she tragically died giving birth to one of their children, he was heartbroken. He asked his architect Ustad Ahmad Lahori to create a magnificent building in her memory, which would be called the TAJ MAHAL.

Show off your skills

Lahori designed a magnificent SHOW-OFF BUILDING for the Shah. He had lots of EPIC IDEAS for how it should look:

- made of bright white marble
- a huge onion-shaped dome on top
- decorated with gold and precious jewels
- surrounded by gardens with mirror-like pools

Success!

The whole project took 20,000 workers 21 YEARS to finish and cost A LOT. But it is one of the world's greatest buildings—NICE WORK, USTAD! It is also a perfect final resting place for Mumtaz and Shah Jahan, who are now buried there together.

ANTONI GAUDI

Gaudí was a Spanish architect who designed buildings like NOTHING seen before. He was a quiet man but his buildings had SPECTACULAR SHOW-OFF STYLE!

Building with IMAGINATION

Gaudí designed houses in the city of Barcelona. His designs used dramatic CURVES, ARCHES, and ANIMAL SHAPES, often covered in BROKEN TILES.

Going BIG

In 1883, Antoni was put in charge of building a large church in Barcelona, called the SAGRADA FAMILIA ("Holy Family"). He made it one of the most SENSATIONAL SHOW-OFF buildings in the WORLD. Gaudí worked for 43 years on the church but when he died it was still only a QUARTER FINISHED. It has been worked on for over 140 years—and it's still not finished today!

Hurry up and finish it, I'm 170 now!

Natural know-how

As a young man, Antoni loved the outdoors. His stunning show-off projects were based on things that he loved in NATURE:

- trees
- wildlife
- mountains
- caves

WILLIAM SHAKESPEARE

Over 400 years ago, an Englishman named Will started acting in theaters. He then wrote plays, and now is probably the most famous writer ever! But was he a SHOW-OFF?

To be or not to be... A SHOW-OFF!

Acting funny

Shakespeare was a good actor and liked showing off his skills on stage. He played heroes, villains, kings, ghosts, and more, wearing FANCY COSTUMES and putting on different voices.

Play time!

William wrote more than 30 plays of his own, and they are still performed today! He wrote funny comedies, sad tragedies, lovey-dovey romances, and history plays about royal families. Have you heard of these plays? They've been performed THOUSANDS of times:

- Romeo and Juliet—they LOVE each other but their families are sworn ENEMIES
- A Midsummer Night's Dream—fairies cause CHAOS in the forest with love spells, silly tricks and...a donkey?!

Wowing audiences

Shakespeare's plays were full of twists, surprises, and clever wordplay, with lots of magical and memorable characters. And people ADORED them—even Queen Elizabeth I and King James I were fans! With some fellow Tudor actors, show-off Shakespeare built HIS OWN THEATER in London, called The Globe, and people crowded in to watch his plays.

OSCAR WILDE

Many 19th-century writers were quiet, modest people who spent a lot of time alone, working away. VERY few were fashionable CELEBS, like the one-of-a-kind Oscar Wilde.

Stylish student

Oscar grew up in Ireland and was an intelligent, funny, artistic boy. He did well at school and then went off to Oxford University, in England. In Victorian times, most students were smartly dressed but Oscar had REALLY LONG HAIR, and wore LOUD CLOTHES and FANCY HATS.

His room in college was full of PEACOCK FEATHERS and BIG FLOWERS. He dared to express himself through his STYLE!

Children's classics

Oscar Wilde wrote some famous stories for children. Try reading one of these and see what you think!

- The Happy Prince
- The Selfish Giant

Witty writer

Oscar was a super-talented writer of poems, stories, and essays. He was FUNNY as well as BRAINY, and people loved seeing his clever, witty plays in London theaters.

He was gay, at a time when this was illegal in England, and he is a very important part of LGBTQIA+ history.

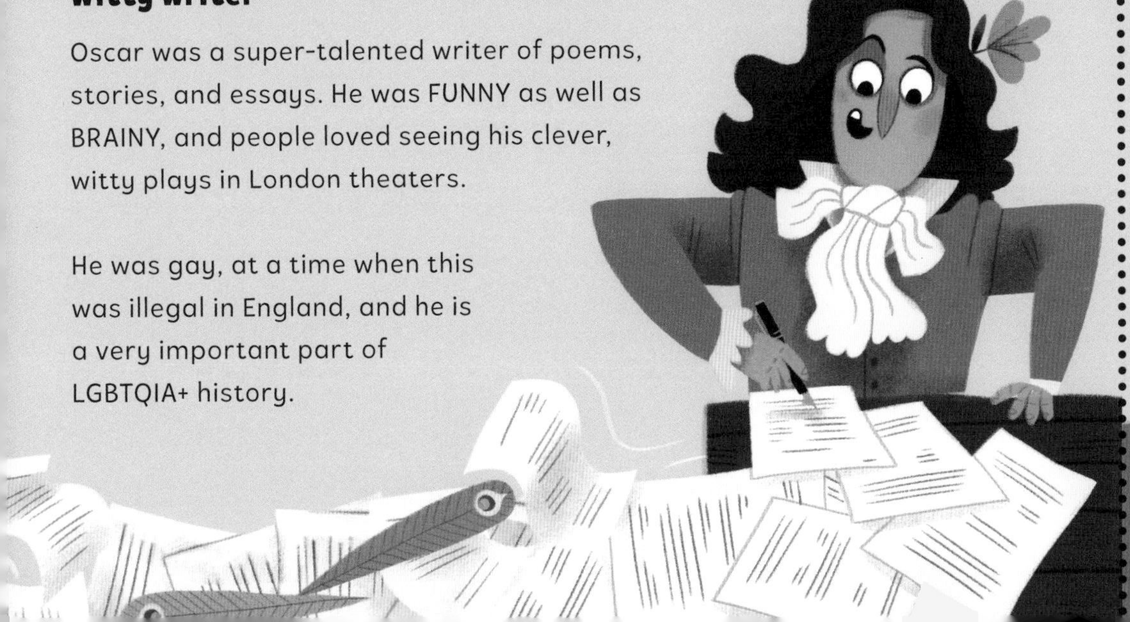

TIMELINE

People have been showing off for THOUSANDS of years! Can you spot who the earliest show-off is? And who lived more recently, Mansa Musa or Marie Curie?

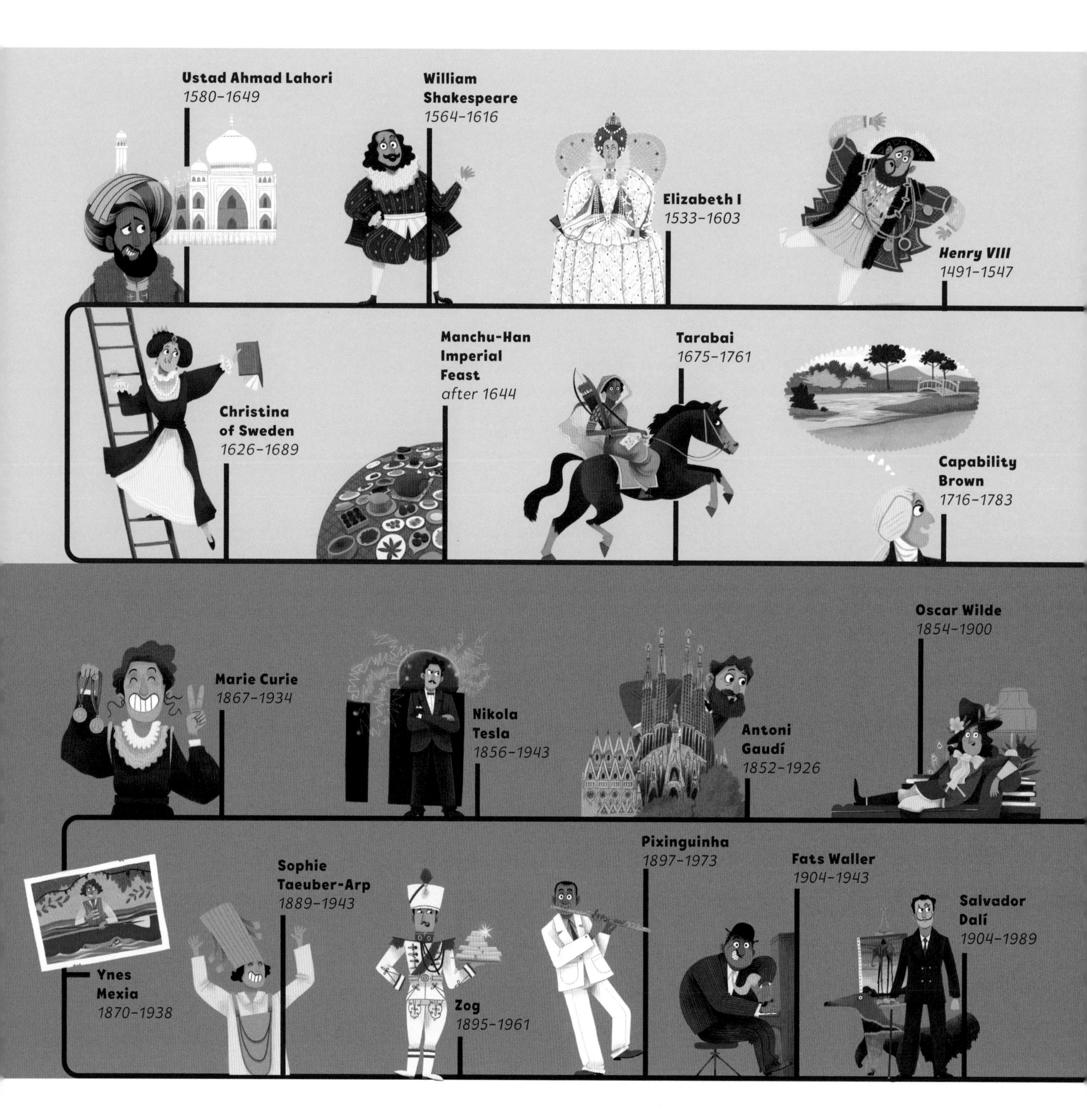

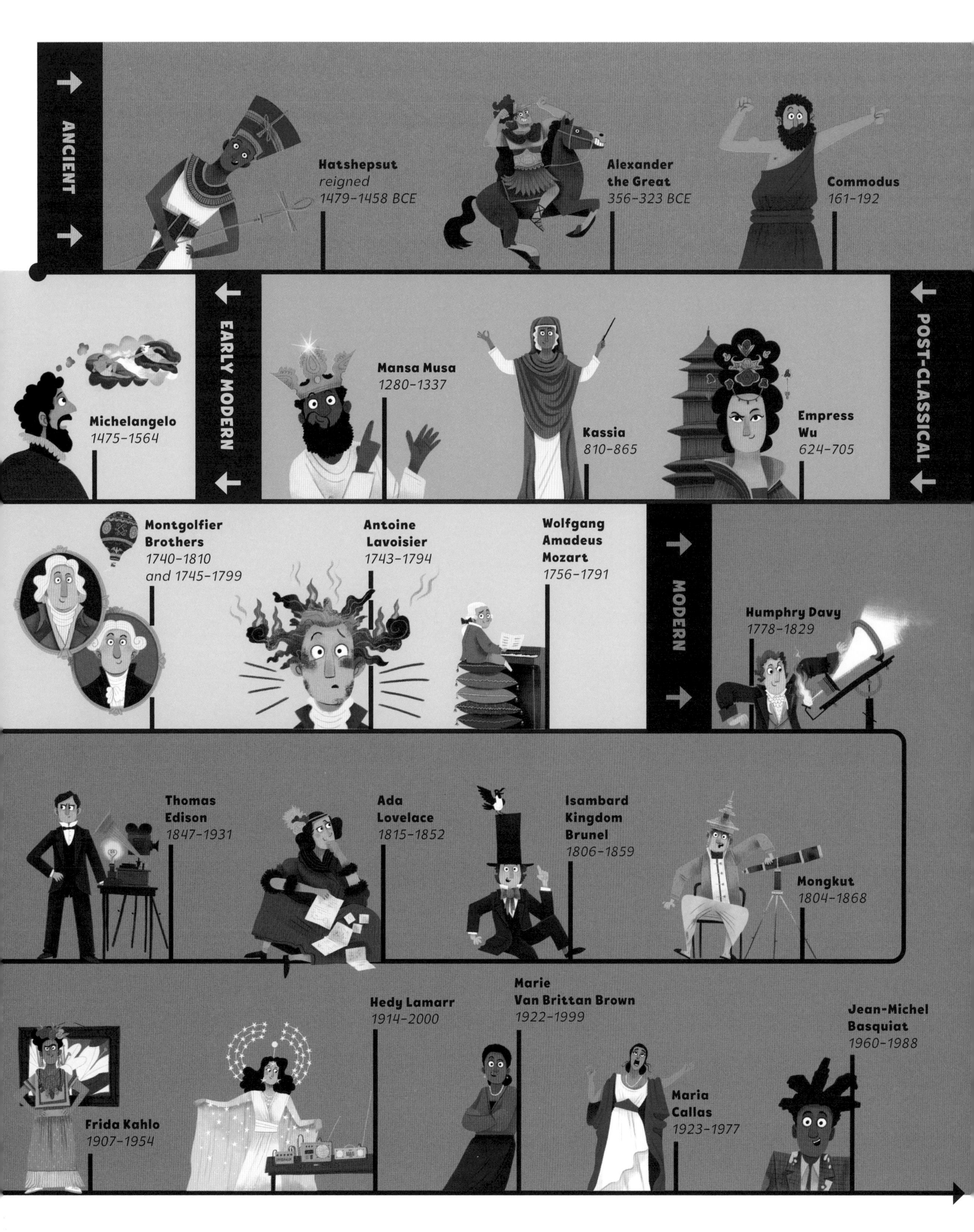
ANCIENT
Hatshepsut
reigned
1479–1458 BCE
Alexander
the Great
356–323 BCE
Commodus
161–192
POST-CLASSICAL
Empress
Wu
624–705
Kassia
810–865
Mansa Musa
1280–1337
EARLY MODERN
Michelangelo
1475–1564
Montgolfier
Brothers
1740–1810
and 1745–1799
Antoine
Lavoisier
1743–1794
Wolfgang
Amadeus
Mozart
1756–1791
MODERN
Humphry Davy
1778–1829
Thomas
Edison
1847–1931
Ada
Lovelace
1815–1852
Isambard
Kingdom
Brunel
1806–1859
Mongkut
1804–1868
Frida Kahlo
1907–1954
Hedy Lamarr
1914–2000
Marie
Van Brittan Brown
1922–1999
Maria
Callas
1923–1977
Jean-Michel
Basquiat
1960–1988

QUIZ ANSWERS

PEOPLE IN CHARGE—WHO'S WHO?, PAGE 8

5 **Hatshepsut** female ruler of ancient Egypt

4 **Zog** luxury-loving king who really liked cake

11 **Henry VIII** king who loved flashy jewelry

8 **Elizabeth I** strong and fashionable queen

6 **Christina** brainy, book-loving queen

1 **Mansa Musa** mega-rich ruler who gave away gold

2 **Mongkut** busy king and stargazer with a big family

3 **Tarabai** brave warrior queen

10 **Wu** empress who wanted power—and got it

7 **Alexander the Great** leader who took over a huge chunk of the world

9 **Commodus** nasty Roman emperor who loved to win

Show-off Rulers, page 24

1. a) spices—although they would have been carried by camels!
2. b) chocolate
3. a) 57 carriages
4. b) massive mustache
5. c) 1,000 suits

Show-off engineers and inventors, page 42

1. c) railway locomotive
2. c) shape-shifting fountains
3. b) robot band that played music
4. b) rode across it with a rooster on her knee
5. c) home security system

PEOPLE WHO THINK UP STUFF—WHO'S WHO?, PAGE 26

6 **Hedy Lamarr** film star and ace tech inventor

4 **Humphry Davy** gave fierce science talks

3 **Montgolfier Brothers** built the first flying machine

2 **Antoine Lavoisier** scientist who discovered the gases oxygen and hydrogen

10 **Isambard K. Brunel** bold engineer who liked to build big things

9 **Nikola Tesla** master of electrical inventions

8 **Thomas Edison** inventor and businessman with lots of ideas

1 **Ada Lovelace** first ever computer programmer

5 **Marie Curie** prize-winning, life-saving super-scientist

7 **Ynes Mexia** plant collector and epic traveler

PEOPLE WHO CREATE THINGS—WHO'S WHO?, PAGE 44

3 **Sophie Taeuber-Arp** multi-talented painter, designer, and craftsperson

9 **Antoni Gaudí** creator of big, colorful buildings

10 **William Shakespeare** writer of some of history's most famous plays

8 **Ustad Ahmad Lahori** architect of the Taj Mahal, a beautiful world wonder

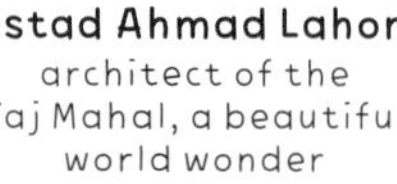

1 **Frida Kahlo** Mexican artist and fashion sensation

6 **Capability Brown** royal gardener and landscape designer

4 **Salvador Dalí** made strange, tricky paintings (and sculptures)

11 **Oscar Wilde** witty, fashionable writer who threw fun parties

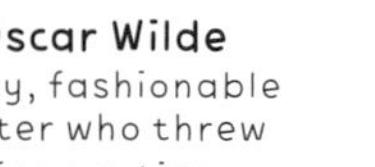

5 **Jean-Michel Basquiat** artist who filled galleries and street walls with art

2 **Michelangelo** amazing painter and sculptor of big, beautiful statues

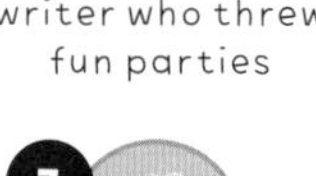

7 **Manchu-Han Imperial Feast chefs** creators of a giant feast

GLOSSARY

architect a person who designs buildings

art movement an approach to making artwork in a certain style, such as Surrealism

banquet a huge, fancy meal held for a special reason

convent a building where nuns live and work

eclipse a solar eclipse is when the Sun is blocked by the Moon

elements substances, such as iron or oxygen, that cannot be broken down into anything else

emperor the ruler of an empire, which is a vast group of lands

empire a large area of land ruled by one person

fort a strong building used for defense against enemies

generator a machine that produces electricity

gorge a very steep, deep, rocky valley

Hajj a special religious journey to Mecca, made by Muslims

heritage someone's or something's past or tradition

Latin the language spoken by the ancient Romans

lecture a talk given by an expert

locomotive an engine that pulls a train

marble a beautiful type of stone, often used for carvings

military to do with war and battles

myth a very old traditional story

pharaoh a ruler of ancient Egypt

radioactivity a kind of invisible, dangerous energy

sculpture a work of art, often carved from stone or wood, that you can see from different sides

soprano a female singer who often sings in operas

species one particular type of living thing

suspension bridge a bridge that hangs from strong cables

symbol a picture or sign that stands for something, such as a dove for peace

symphony a long, complicated piece of music for lots of instruments

temple a building used for worship

trade buying and selling things

Tudor a time in British history, from 1485 to 1603

witty funny in a clever way

INDEX